CHRISTMAS ANGELS WHISPER

CHRISTMAS ANGELS WHISPER

A Christmas Story

David L. Asay

ELM HILL

A Division of
HarperCollins Christian Publishing

www.elmhillbooks.com

Christmas Angels Whisper
A Christmas Story

Published in Nashville, Tennessee, by Elm Hill, an imprint of Thomas Nelson. Elm Hill and Thomas Nelson are registered trademarks of HarperCollins Christian Publishing, Inc.

Elm Hill titles may be purchased in bulk for educational, business, fund-raising, or sales promotional use. For information, please e-mail SpecialMarkets@ ThomasNelson.com.

Library of Congress Cataloging-in-Publication Data

Library of Congress Control Number: 2018930966

ISBN 978-1-595547040 (PB)
ISBN 978-1-595546968 (HC)
ISBN 978-1-595547729 (eBook)

TABLE OF CONTENTS

FOREWORD

An argument could be made that in life there are certain action-able dates that become actionable simply because many choices and previous events in time pointed to a certain forthcoming date with destiny or atrocity. For example, a number of events culminated in an actionable date that we celebrate as July 4, 1776. Veteran's Day was an actionable date because many previous events pointed to the day when it actually was realized.

Some families have certain "actionable dates." It could be the parents' anniversary, for example. Other actionable dates could mark a turning point in a history of a family and there were a number of circumstances or events that led to that specific date. Often it becomes the date itself that gets the remembrance and seldom any thought gets placed on the circumstances and events that preceded it.

Wanda Briggs Asay died on February 19, 1968. She was almost forty-three years old. That's what appears on the record, but there is more to the story in realizing the events surrounding a two-year battle with cancer. There were highs and lows, miracles and meltdowns. Within there is a Christmas celebration that deserves remembrance more than the bare statistic of another person dying of cancer.

In her husband's journal, there is a notation of something that happened during the Christmas season of 1967. Basil Asay wasn't very specific; he rarely was a man of copious descriptions except in telling stories and he never told a story to his grandchildren of Christmas 1967. The story needs to be told for the sake of those who have battled a deadly disease and wondered why. It needs to be told for the sake of the children who were literally a miracle and that the miracle of those five children probably cost her life in the balance.

That which achieves a high worth in a person's core will get qualified for its high placement and oftentimes there is a price placed to determine how valuable that commodity may be. Wanda Asay wanted to be a mother more than any other calling and there was a price exacted to determine how dear she held that commission. It had a promise made to her by an old patriarch and she wrote of how sacred that was in her journal. The promise would be realized! Little do most people realize the price tag associated with the job description of a mother.

Cancer mortality rates have gone down significantly over the last forty years. Cervical cancer is much more understood than it was earlier when it ranked second in cancer deaths among women. Certain medical treatments in the 1960s actually contributed to cervical cancer. Vaccinations, checkups, and tests have significantly reduced the possibility of death from cervical cancer in the present day. The problem would continue to be that the disease could metastasize to bone or other tissues before it was ever caught. It was a tediously painful way to leave this life.

PROLOGUE

July 20, 1966
Middle of Night

Now that was really weird! It must be around 3:00 a.m. and all of a sudden the stairway light came on. At our house, the boys slept in the basement. Four boys sharing two rooms. I shared a room with Dale. Lights just don't come on in the wee hours of the night and I wondered why it even disturbed me. I had to tell myself, "David, you're dreaming. Turn over and get back to sleep."

I was about ready to comply when suddenly it was just my vision playing tricks on me; now it was sound and another sense. Something wasn't right! It would have been bad enough that a deepening feeling of dread and peril felt like a weight on my chest. Something in the universe of my little house and bedroom was way out of harmony and the feeling was practically palpable. The sound that accompanied the heavy feeling put me way beyond sleep. Something was coming down the stairs and they were not being quiet about it.

Our home was probably built in the early 1940s with a high-pitched roof and old wooden shake shingles. The back door on the outside opened on the driveway on the east side of the house. On the inside was a slight landing and then an opening to the right went into the kitchen and the opening straight ahead went directly downstairs. The stairs were creaky and covered in old linoleum. There was no mistaking that whatever had come into the house was coming downstairs and there was no creaking about the descent. It was loud and purposeful.

Bountiful, Utah, in the 1960s was really a small place between the bigger cities of Salt Lake and Ogden. Nothing bad ever passed through Bountiful. People didn't even lock their doors most of the time. We didn't lock our bikes even, just parked them in the driveway. About the worst that ever happened was hearing the fire engines running off to put out a brush fire or maybe some teen hoodlums doing a bit of vandalism to a rival school's mascot. Something big was coming down the stairs in my house. The feeling was intense, the fear was palpable!

To get to my room required a left turn at the bottom of the stairs. Dale and I slept in the room on the left and Alan and Grant had the room across the hall from ours. Whatever had come down the stairs was not being quiet about it and surely my brothers had heard or felt something. In the few seconds it took for a decision to be made by this intruder, I had again questioned if this were a dream. It was loud and vivid and if I had known what adrenaline was, I was sure I had released a gallon. There is no way that this was a dream! I was awake!

Which way would the intruder turn? Maybe he would venture on to the family room or what if he went into our haunted "fruit room" under the stairs. The witches who we knew lived in there would surely take care of the visitor. It's true we had vivid imaginations and maybe indulged in a couple of spook shows, but this wasn't a story and it wasn't a dream. Something unwanted was there in the basement and had likely come in through the unlocked back door.

It was dark in my room and I had turned to face the door with my head still glued to my pillow. I could see the shadow at the base of the stairs and a few survival instincts seemed to kick in as I evaluated options. There was no way I could get out of the tiny window in our room. A house built in the 1940s didn't have egress codes for windows in bedrooms. I could scream and throw off the covers and then what?! This shadowy intruder covered the only way out. Were any of my brothers seeing this and sharing what I feel? I glanced over at Dale and he looked sound asleep. I sure wish that I was. But how could he be asleep with the light and the noise. Why am I awake?

As the entity sensed something and started to turn, I reacted in a split second and turned my head up on the pillow with my eyes closed and in full sleep mode. Some ferocious animals, I was told somewhere in cub scouts or something, wouldn't attack if you played dead and I thought sleeping was the next best thing. What predator would attack and dismember a sleeping little kid, right?!

Just as if on some unseen cue, the intruder turned fully to the left and stood in my doorway. It wasn't that my eyes were open to see him pause there in the doorway, but I knew. There was a distinct pattern in breathing that had come from some exertion prior. I could hear the breathing so I knew he was coming my way and wasn't taking any of the other excellent choices that might have found him in a witches brew or exploring the family room and allowing me to escape upstairs and out. Of all of the choices possible—my room.

There was no doubt from the breathing that this was a male of the species. The breathing was low and deeper than any female I had ever heard. He came on into the room and was headed to my bed as if some sixth sense had alerted him to the reality that I was the only one awake and conscious of his trespass. No other sounds, just the breathing. Now he was right by my bedside and the overpowering feeling of dread was intense and I saw no relief and certainly no escape.

He stood over me looking down for what seemed like several minutes. The smell came to my nostrils and it wasn't a pleasant smell. It was fetid and gross and I sure hoped that he couldn't sense my skin crawl as I laid there waiting for the inevitable. To be sure, I was good at playing the sleeping child. I had practiced many time with my parents, particularly on a Christmas Eve and I knew how a body looked and breathed in slumber. How long could I pull this off?

As I lay there, I had a moment to again make sure that I was awake and that this boy wasn't dreaming. I went through a small self-awareness quiz to make sure that I wasn't sleeping such as telling my left toe to go taut and then relax. I could feel in my mind that this wasn't a dream. So if not a dream, what was this!!?? I thought about my racing heart. More proof that this wasn't a dream, but would my intruder notice it? Not much I could do about pure fear and a racing heartbeat and nowhere to hide.

I'm just a kid; I can't help it and boys have this acute curiosity. I lay there and I pretended sleep, but my senses were on alert and the heavy and low breathing was simply challenging me to look. I had never heard anyone breathe like this. Deep, low, and almost raspy. Too many minutes to lie here pretending—I had to do something! I remembered hearing somewhere that there is this condition called "rapid eye movement" when a person is asleep. Apparently their eyeballs don't remain fixed and unmoving, but I had never watched a person sleeping to see if this was true. I had reached a point after several minutes of this thing staring at me.

I wasn't not about to be killed without at least seeing what got me. No way! Apparently it wasn't leaving after determining that I was asleep. Or maybe he really wanted me to wake up and fix on that face as the last thing that I would see before being horribly dismembered. A ten-year-old boy can conjure up incredible ways to check out of this life. Lying there, I came up with a plan. I had to satisfy my curiosity, but I didn't want it to know and have the satisfaction of that being my final view on checking out of this life.

I had also practiced and mastered the gradual "closed eye" squint. A person could actually keep the eyelids closed to a point where the lashes could still practically touch and yet the eye could look out for a second or two in a slow leisurely opening and closing. I rationalized that this could be part of "rapid eye movement" or at least mistaken for that although I had my doubts whether this unwelcome visitor had any idea about "rapid eye movement" or how that would be taken.

Now was the time to test it. I had the advantage of the shadow as he stood over me in my bed and in the darkness, I told myself that he would not notice my eyes slowing opening a tiny crack as long as my eyelashes still held position of closed. Ever so slowly I began the process. Both eyes operating synchronously and opening to a slit in a darkened room.

Oh, to be sure I saw it. I could never forget what I saw enveloped in the shadows but all the more real. The light from the open doorway and stairway beyond gave sufficient light to see that my intruder was hairy and huge. Broad shoulders framed the creature and the huge head was close to shoulders as if there wasn't a neck. It was too dark to see facial features because the light was behind. I had seen enough. It was seared into my mind and I gradually closed my eyes and accepted whatever fate was going to come.

I could feel a loathing and hatred for me in that moment. Did that have something to do with my sight? The heavy feeling was still there, but something more had been added. Whatever it was, gorilla or beast from hell, it didn't like me and wanted my destruction. Prayer was the only thing that I had and I exercised it in my mind.

After several minutes, it simply turned and made its way to the stairs and left the same way that it entered. As I pondered the whole event, I figured that I had just been visited by death or some demon dedicated to destruction. No one else had experienced what I had and I questioned everyone the next day. The light stayed on all night. What was the meaning of this visit? Did it mean something really bad was coming towards me and my family? Had the angel of death stopped by to let me know that it was laying claim to something or someone in this house?

CHAPTER 1

August 1, 1966
Bountiful, Utah

Summer was the amazing time of year! That would be true unless the garden needed weeding or the peaches needed picking. But there was the promise of birthday cake later today, because missing Ellen's birthday was not an option. Six years old and princess of the spoiled brats. We wouldn't be seeing her out pulling weeds in the garden. Oh no, she was taking care of her dolls and probably having a little tea party with her imaginary friends.

It wasn't that we all didn't love our baby sister, but there was only so much of Daddy's favoritism that we could swallow. All four of us older boys were out sweating in the garden thinning beets or pulling weeds. Alan had the assignment to dig up some potatoes. It was Monday, the day after the day of rest. Really funny! Day of Sweat should be the name. I had the privilege of picking the peaches and putting them in a basket. I was sure we would be bottling peaches before the week was over and that would be torture. Dale and Grant were over pulling weeds and I think they threw more clods at each other than pulling weeds. They were a couple years littler and could be expected not to take the chores as seriously.

But if Mom came out and caught them, yes, that would be a sight to watch from a distance! It wasn't that Mom was known for a temper or anything, but chores were chores and she expected that to happen. Mom was tall and thin and she held a firm line with her children as her father had with her. Grandpa Briggs just lived two houses up Center Street and he knew about work as well.

Here we were five children and most of us working our butts off. We knew there would be a little time for a break today because Mom had a doctor appointment again and that meant we could skip off and ride bikes or even have a tomato fight with some of those juicy and rotten tomatoes we forgot to pick last week. Just another hour of this torture and we would be free for a while.

This was Mom's second doctor visit. Seemed like she was just at the doctor last week. I didn't even know she was sick or maybe she was pregnant again. It's been quite a few years since Ellen was born, but it could be possible. If it was confirmed she would probably tell us. She had always told us when she was expecting another addition and she told us of the miracle that it was for her to have children.

Mom had been told around 1948 or 1949 that she wasn't going to have children. They told her that she only had a fourth of an ovary or some such small percentage of an ovary and we had to look up what that meant in the encyclopedia. I guess ovaries produce an egg and that's necessary to make a baby, but I sure didn't want to go into that detail even if I had to read *National Geographic*.

Well, Mom had been told in a special blessing that she had received when she was a young lady that she would be a mother and now this doctor said that she wouldn't be a mother. This was devastating, but it wasn't going to fly with her because she had this thing called "faith" and the promise made to her. Five kids from a quarter ovary is pretty good proof about who was right and it still made Dr. D smile.

About this time, a devious thought crossed my mind as I picked those peaches. Dale and Grant were having a pretty good time slinging clods at each other and I didn't see any consequences coming. What harm would it be if I found a juicy rotten peach way up high in this tree that the birds wouldn't even peck at? What harm could I do (from hiding) if I launched that peach in a high arch straight over and down exploding between those two lazy boys?! That would be spectacular and even better if they got some goop on them.

The throw was nearly perfect from a guy in training to be a pitcher. Splat down right near Dale and the shock on his face was priceless. He couldn't tell which tree was the hiding place and I was fairly protected up there and laughing quietly. But he knew who did it and I was fairly sure that he had a bit of revenge in his mind. Grant had been surprised, but he was fairly sure my aim was for Dale and not him.

Dale wasn't a squealer and it was unlikely that he would risk leaving his post just in case Mom would catch him hunting me down with a muddy old clod and away from his assigned weeding. On the other hand, Dale could have a temper and rotten peach slime was surely a catalyst. Anger and a wee bit of adrenaline gave me my answer. He would risk coming for me and my smile faded as I planned my next move. Several other peach projectiles looked promising and so did escape.

Making a run for it was promising and I didn't want to be trapped in a tree. I wasn't about to back off either, so I grabbed a couple of prizewinning puke peaches and dropped out of hiding. It took less than two seconds to balance and chuck my P. Bombs and then I was running toward the far side of the house. At least one of my bombs hit home with a pleasing smack, but I was long gone. I could hear Grant whooping with laughter. Alan was still working hard at the potato harvest.

Dale was now red-hot angry. I wanted to get more ammunition, but I had to choose my battles. In these brotherly games, you better believe that sportsmanship was out the window. A couple of clods flew over my left shoulder as I juked to the right and ran on. Coming around the front yard, I heard a sound I had not been anticipating:

"Dale, where are you!!?"

"David, come and bring in your basket."

"Where are you kids?!"

Dale froze. He was clearly not in the garden and Grant was there working hard and gaining brownie points. Dale would have to come up with something and Mom could spot a lie quicker than a potgut could go down his hole. I was even farther away at the front of the house. Dale was the first one back and reported in. He smelled and looked like a splatted peach. He didn't have to tell Mom what had happened and who had done it. This was a no-brainer for superMom.

"David, get over here right now!!"

I had been prepared with the excuse of going to the garage to get another basket, but we both knew that wasn't going to hold water. I skulked over to her from the patio and she stood there with her hands on her hips trying to devise some appropriate punishment while Dale looked like the saint of peach puke.

"So this is what you do when you are supposed to be working!? You get on in the house and sit on a chair for a half hour and then I'm going to think up some appropriate punishment and we're not through with this! I swear I don't know what gets into you sometime!"

For my part, I hated being punished with sitting on a chair. I'd rather pick peaches. But I was benched and Dale just smiled and headed back to his weed-pulling. Mom caught on to that and brought him up short: "Dale, you get over to the hose and wash that filth off of you and then get back in the house and change. Let's add another half hour to your weed-pulling experience as well to make up for the lost time."

All in all, I fared quite well that time. I got chair duty and Dale got weeds. But I got the huge satisfaction of connecting with Dale on that spectacular rotten peach. Probably worth it, right? Mom would be leaving for her appointment soon and freedom would be mine. "Not too shabby, David."

CHAPTER 2

August 1, 1966
Bountiful, Utah

That evening we celebrated Ellen's birthday. She got a few more presents; nothing that I really cared for. I did like that new record that she got for her portable record player. I knew she'd wear out "Puff the Magic Dragon" from someone named Peter, Paul, and Mary, but it was a neat song too.

Cake and homemade ice cream were a real treat. We sang "Happy Birthday" like we meant it and I suppose we did. She was our little sis and she was a princess. She beamed like this was the best birthday ever. We also went up to see Grandpa Briggs and Aunt Phoebe up the street and shared the birthday cake with them. Then the grownups sat down in the living room to talk. We stayed nearby and listened to the radio while catching little bits of grownup talk.

I remember some talk of the latest news and that some guy had climbed on top of a tower in Texas and started shooting people. That was crazy and my parents wondered what the world was coming to. After a little bit, the talk got a bit of a different tone and I really cued in when Mom said, "Well, I got my results from Dr. Diumenti today and I've got to tell you."

For the next three minutes, she unloaded the diagnosis and it wasn't a pregnancy. The diagnosis was something called "cervical cancer" and it had been very hard to detect because it really wasn't felt until it became pretty deeply entrenched. The medical professionals would probably like Mom to go to LDS hospital in Salt Lake and get a biopsy (whatever that was) and then decide what to do from that point.

It didn't sound good. I hadn't heard this "cancer" word before, but it sounded really ominous when they said it. Maybe that was what Grandma Briggs had died of shortly after I was born. One thing for sure, the mood of everyone got really solemn, like we were in church and some boring old guy was talking. I could tell something was really dreadful and it reminded me of a feeling I had a couple of weeks ago in my bedroom when that gorilla had come calling.

I was determined to look this up in the encyclopedia when I got home, but right when we arrived home, Dad called us all into the living room and sat us down. This couldn't be good. This only happened prior to punishment and a serious talk from Dad was not a good thing. He began his little chat:

"Kids, we are facing a bit of a hard time coming. Mom has just been diagnosed with cancer and that's not something to fool around with, but we can get through this. Now cancer is a bad bug that's got rooted down there in the mommy area and it has been really hard to tell what was wrong because up until recently, it hasn't been painful. Now Mom can start to feel it. We can do some things to try to kill it, but that's pretty hard on the body and so Mom will be really weak."

Mom added a few comments too: "This is just another challenge for us. We came through just fine when all those doctors told me that I wouldn't have children and now I have you five wonderful kids. They will probably first want to take out my mommy parts in surgery and that's called a hysterectomy. They might operate on other things to try to get all of this disease out of me. We can do this thing and then we'll get back on top of things. Daddy, do you want to tell the kids what we have planned for starting next year?"

Dad replied, "Well, we have just purchased a lot up the street. I bought the east lot and my buddy at the building department bought the west lot. We're going to build a house and move up there into a brand-new house. It's going to be amazing and you will have your own rooms. You get to help me build it and this house will be very cool."

Finally some good news in all of this. Building a house sounds like fun. Getting my own room is especially impressive. But this cancer thing was still a bit of a concern especially because of that feeling that I had. Was the gorilla stalking me again? I knew that I had to check it out.

Our encyclopedia had a lot of information. Cancer was a bad thing and it was a leading cause of death. The cure rate wasn't impressive and this thing called the "mortality rate" meant that it killed many more than got away from it. Surgery was the first mode of attack and in cutting out all the bad stuff, they hoped that it wouldn't go anywhere else. Then there was this procedure called chemotherapy where they put some medicine in a person that kills off practically every cell whether good or bad cells and then the person had to recover from that.

That night I shared my knowledge with my brothers and that this cancer thing was a killer. The problem was that you might kill it, but then again it might have snuck into another area and comes alive all over again. If it got into some really vital organ, then it was all over. Mom had proven the doctors wrong before and here were her miracle children to beat all the odds and medical statistics. Mom had five children. The odds were huge against that, but she was promised to have children and she did. We said our prayers and went to sleep that evening fairly confident that this would be over soon and we would have a new house on top of it all.

I found out later that Mom and Dad talked late into the night. Alone with their thoughts, they faced the reality that this was serious. People didn't usually make it through cancer. Why did this happen? Mom wondered what she had done wrong to deserve this judgment. How could she continue to be a mother and attend to her *Sweet Adelines'* duties. This *Sweet Adelines* group was a prominent choral group of women in

Bountiful and she loved her participation. She felt that this was all over and that this was somehow a price that she had to pay.

Dad reassured her that it was going to be all right. He reminded her that we had this house to look forward to and they spent some time discussing the plans and what they wanted in their new house. There were some new styles that were gaining popularity and some new gadgets that could be built into kitchen cabinets. They could design their own master suite and some fantastic innovations in closets. Dad, to his credit, tried to refocus on the positive, but we all knew Mom and what remained in the back of her mind wasn't easily persuaded to leave.

CHAPTER 3

September 1, 1967
Bountiful, Utah

What an eventful summer it has been! This is actually my last free day before school starts in four days and I've got big things planned with friends for our last break before school on Monday. I actually start sixth grade and I'm in the same class as my best friend, Jeff Goodrich. It's going to be the best year. We're probably going to be moving into the new house and I'll have my own room. Life couldn't get much better now that the hard part of building a house was over and we were set for school to start.

On that deal with Mom, that was still an up and down thing. Seems like it was mostly down. They don't talk much about it, but I can tell that Mom is losing heart. She doesn't smile much, she doesn't sew much. She had to quit her singing group and she seems pretty weak most of the time. They got her this walker device after she came back from her latest stay in the hospital. She can't seem to get around much anymore and although she puts on the happy face when we're around, we know enough about Mom to know that she's faking it.

It's been just over a year since we got the news. Several operations later and more doctor visits than I care to count. Quiet talks with grownups so that we don't know anything. My aunts spend more time visiting and Mom spends more time in bed. I thought we were supposed to be looking forward to moving into the new house and that life would be rosy again like before. Mom could come out and yell at us for peach fights or tomato wars. I could be grounded on a kitchen chair for hours if I could have that life back again.

But hold that thought. I'm going to be a cool sixth grader! Most groovy! I'm a popular kid in my grade and I have good friends. I don't much like girls, but if I was pressed, I might admit an infatuation with Janet. Boy stuff is cool and riding bikes is the best! Playing football and kick the can at the neighborhood level is radical fun and I'm good not getting mushy with girls because they have fleas and everyone knows that. (Well maybe Janet is the exception.) Today I'm going riding with my friends up in the mountains above the school. Life is grand!

I am just getting my bike ready to go meet up with my friends and head out on this adventure when Ellen comes out to the driveway and tells me that Mom wants to see me. She knows that I have plans and this is really inconvenient, but the least I could do is to go and tell her good bye and that I'll be back later this afternoon. She knows that I've been looking forward to this and she wants me to have this break before school starts.

I head back to her bedroom. My parents have a neat bedroom that my dad added onto the back of the house two years ago. She has been down in bed for a number of days now. She says she is too weak to get up and use her walker. I sort of wonder if that medicine that she takes is causing this weakness or if it's the cancer still. They took practically all of her female stuff away in surgeries and she's thin as a rail and fairly pale. She's still my mom and has that twinkle in her blue eyes when she sees me.

She signals me over to the bed and I approach with a little trepidation and a little hurry to get this visit over with and on my way to the fun stuff. This stuff here is really a drag. (Geez! Now I'm starting to talk like a Hippie!)

"Hi Mom. How ya doing?"

"Hi Son. You know I've always called you Blackie. You'll always be my little Blackie."

Now to be quite honest, I didn't much care for the nickname, but what am I gonna say to my mom here in bed. The next-door neighbors call me Butch and that isn't really impressing me either. So if Mom wants to call me Blackie, that's going to be me. She reaches out her hand for me to take it so she can pull me a little closer.

"Come on over here and sit with me on the bed for a little bit. Tell me what you're up to."

Oh my gosh, surely I don't have time for this. I've got to finish my bike check and get down the road! Yikes, this could take a while.

"Well, Mom, here's the deal. I'm heading over to meet up with Jeff and Tim and we're going up into the hills for a bike adventure like I talked about last night with you. This is really cool. I've got my lunch packed and I'm just checking over my bike before I go."

"That sounds exciting, Blackie. Before you go, can I ask a little favor and then go and have a great time?"

"Sure Mom, just say the word. What can I do?" I hope I don't sound too hurried as I reply.

"Can you just give me a little kiss before you go? I can't remember the last time you gave me a little kiss and told me that you loved me. You were probably five years old last time, right?"

I am probably stammering as I try to think of a really cool reply because I am a really cool kid. So I haltingly respond: "Gee, Mom.... Well.... You know don't you that I'm almost twelve years old?"

"And?" she looks at me a bit perplexed with those twinkly blue eyes.

"It's not anything really. It's...you know.... It's a kid thing. Boys don't kiss girls and I know that you're my mom and all, but cool kids just don't do that. We got a code."

"Son, it's we 'have' a code and I get it. It just seems like a long time since I got one and I am your mom."

"Yeah, I got that and I have a code. But I'm *cool* and if the other kids found out that I kissed my mom, I'd never hear the end of it. You understand, don't you?" The words just stumble out and it is really awkward.

"Well then, have a great ride. Sorry to have bothered you. You are a cool kid and I wouldn't want to mess that up with a little thing like a kiss."

I am free! Get me outta here! Talk about awkward!! What got into her with that request? But I AM COOL! Cool kids don't kiss their mom and certainly not any girl. That is just yucky and I want no part of that. I tried it once with my cousin and that was disgusting. There are just some things that you don't do and maintain a good reputation and coolness. I am glad to be out of that situation.

As I leave on my bike, I wonder if I would remember this experience in years to come or if I would remember the spectacular bike ride I am going to have. Part of me feels a little guilty at turning my mom's request down. The other part of me shrugs it off as an unfair request of a 'cool' kid and I am off to new adventures.

CHAPTER 4

October 7, 1967
Bountiful, Utah

It's Saturday and no school. The weather is beginning to turn and Halloween is coming up. That's always a fun time. Our neighborhood really gets into that holiday. There's this real craze for the show *Outer Limits* and Jeff has planned to dress up like an alien. I don't know what I want to be yet. Alan told us that he's not going out this year. Suddenly he's too old. Oh well, I'm cool and in my prime. Sixth graders can really have a blast and maybe we'll do some really nasty prank on Mrs. Houser if she doesn't give us something good this year.

I've always loved the autumn time of year. The weather has cooled and leaves are turning and falling. There's football and holidays and great things happen in this season. Christmas is coming and that's my favorite time. All things look better through Christmas eyes and Christmas presents.

Dale, Grant, and I stayed up late last night and watched *Nightmare Theatre* and it was particularly scary for a change. Something about fearless Vampire killers, but I'm not sure about the title. We all slept in and then we got the duty of raking leaves for a few hours, feeding the rabbits, and winterizing around the garden and yard. There are always chores.

Lately, those Viewmont High School Hoods have been seen around the neighborhood and if they come trolling tonight, Jeff, Tim, and I may be ready with some rotten egg cocktail for them. They have been terrorizing the neighborhood right after their homecoming and they think they are so cool that we sometimes have to show them that the sixth graders can still handle anything that comes from Viewmont.

Last week they chased us clear through our backyard after we shared with them a literal smattering of piss when they stopped us to pick on us. Luckily we know our neighborhood and where to hide and what traps are ready for them. They are far too visible running around in their V lettermen jackets. They never really appreciated our referring to them as the dudettes from Vomit High. No sense of humor I guess.

They were always looking for the punk kids in our neighborhood and felt that it was some rite of passage to pick on sixth graders. I sort of figured that they had single digit IQ's and little else to do in their miserable neighborhoods. Tonight would probably be no different as they trolled the area looking for something to vandalize or kids to torment.

By the time the evening rolled around, it looked like a storm was coming in from the lake and darkness came earlier than usual. We settled in for a night with the television in the living room. By the time it got to Lawrence Welk, we started to think that Mom would join us since that was one of her favorites. She would probably brave the walker to come on out to the living room.

At about five minutes to 7:00 that evening, we heard something fall toward the back of the house. Immediately Dad could tell it was the walker and he jumped up and headed for the back of the house where he found our mother lying on the bedroom floor and writhing in pain. We didn't go back there; Alan kept us there in the living room. Dad got her back on the bed and through her tears, he knew and felt that something had broken inside of her.

He came out briefly to use the kitchen phone and called for an ambulance to come. That was unheard of. We never heard of anyone calling for an ambulance so this was really bad. He immediately went back to the bedroom and tried to attend to stabilizing her but it was an intense situation and we didn't know what to do just sitting there in the living room.

After about fifteen minutes the ambulance arrived and we let the attendants come in with the stretcher. Still we didn't know what was going on or if Mom was even okay. It was a hard time for kids to be left without anything but their imaginations to conjure up gruesome alternatives. Presently they brought the stretcher down the hall and Mom was aboard and sort of raised up. We could tell she was in unimaginable pain, but through it all she was embarrassed that her children had to see her in this way and being wheeled out of the house and carted away.

Dad instructed Alan to watch us and to call Grandpa and Aunt Maxine and tell them they were going to the St. Marks hospital. Dad left and followed the ambulance in his car. We sat there a bit shell-shocked at how fast this evening had gone downhill. It should have been like practically any other night and now Mom was carted off and we had no idea if she was even coming back.

Alan did his best as big brother, but this was beyond his element and he knew as much as we did. The television was still on, but we each kept our own silent vigil for the next few hours hoping for some news. One thing was abundantly clear and the realization was deep and penetrating. Mom wasn't getting better and she probably would never get better. It was serious when an ambulance came to your house and the reality of where we were came with painful clarity.

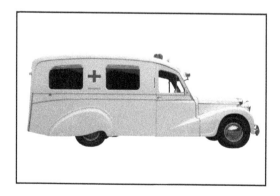

We had held faith that this was a rather long but a passing illness. We were never told anything different and we believed what we were told and just looked forward to a happier time when all would be well again. Our shared reality sank in deep that evening that this vile cancer was not going away and that it would rob us of our mother and that was just not right, just not fair.

Our bubble of hope burst that night and the dread returned. We didn't know if she would come home ever again and we all thought the worst as we sat alone in the living room. For a long time words didn't have to be spoken. We had seen it in full color. When words were finally ventured, it was full blown pity party mode and we didn't understand why this was happening to us. We didn't sign up for this!

I thought back to her request for a kiss barely a month ago and that I had denied her that simple request. I thought of why God would grant miracles in her life and to be a mother of five children and then to rob her of raising them. I thought of what that would mean to me. It wasn't fair, there is nothing right in all of this. Why would God allow his loving daughter and faithful person to be dealt with in such a fashion? We all hurt that evening. Reality was heartless.

Dad came home after several hours. He told us that Mom was heavily sedated and resting. Initial X-rays taken showed that she had fractured her right hip. Her bones were so brittle from the therapy and fighting the disease and the spread of the disease. We asked him to be a bit up front with us because we have imagined everything terrible and that she was never coming home. He admitted that their agreement had been to keep the nature of the illness away from the children so that we could have a more normal life.

We were heading into the holidays now and as parents they wanted us to enjoy the season and live a normal life. We let Dad know that all of this had just gone out the window and let's not be this way anymore. We would take whatever comes, but don't feed us false hope.

I suppose that Dad was at his emotional end as well and his next words would remain with all of us, but we already sort of knew and he needed to say the words so we could move forward:

"Your mom was recently diagnosed with bone cancer. The cancer was not resolved from the surgery and the therapy, and she really can't undergo any further chemo treatments. Her bones are brittle and cannot really support her weight. The cancer is now spreading and once it gets to the liver and major organs and finishes its work there, she will pass away. We didn't want that to be what you were told, but that is the reality.

"It is true that we built a house with the full intent of making our home and new start and getting this behind us. I'm afraid that's not going to happen and I don't know when this will be over. Your mom is more devastated than I've ever seen her. There is not a night that goes by when she doesn't cry and wish that God would give her answers and peace. We don't know why this has happened. She still thinks it's some sort of payback, but God doesn't work with that scorecard. She finds no peace in the realization that she will not be there to raise you guys. She feels no peace and the comfort isn't there.

"We will have to sell that house and we will have to go on. I think that we have a buyer and we will have to pursue that option because I can't see any other way and I'm too tired and drained. I'm sorry to have to express that. You kids are my world and we need to pull together now and make the coming season a real memory and let's make it a good one for her sake.

"They are going to keep her for a couple of weeks. That's my best guess. They will try to patch up the bone and pin it, but she will not walk again. That's what I've been told. She can't support the weight and you can see that there's very little weight left with her. We need to pray that she finds the peace and comfort she needs and that she feels that we are behind her and lift up our happy faces for the coming time. She will not want to see downcast eyes because she will only blame herself and there is no peace in that."

With those few words, it was confirmed that life would not be the same, but we could resolve to put our best faces forward and give her feelings of love and comfort.

I felt for my dad as well. He had always respected the actor Lorne Greene on *Bonanza*. Ben Cartwright faced tremendous challenges and threats to his family. We could have been watching that show tonight. Ben faced incredible setbacks each episode and always came out on top. His family was stalwart and he was in control and he could make anything come out "smellin' like a rose."

There wasn't a Ben Cartwright solution and though my dad had been born in the same year as Lorne Greene and had fairly the same temperament in dealing with trials, that's where the similarity would end when it came to facing this challenge. No one was riding in to save the day. The Asay home wasn't the Ponderosa.

CHAPTER 5

November 23, 1967
Bountiful, Utah

Winter, it seemed, came earlier this year. Some blame it on the "lake effect" snow that attacked the benches of Bountiful with a vengeance. Last night, compounded with a cruel evening easterly, we had heavy snow clinging to the limbs of our pine trees lining the driveway. The weight of this early wet snow threatened to snap even the larger limbs. These trees had endured twenty tough winters and had proven stalwart, but even I had to wonder if this year's unseasonably early burden didn't signal a bleak and dismal winter.

I was sure that my dad felt much like those trees. The burden of what he had told us the month before and spending many hours in the hospital were threatening to overwhelm him until he snapped. But today was Thanksgiving and this wasn't about being burdened or snapped. It was about gratitude and being thankful for our blessings. I, for one, was grateful that Mom was home and would be enjoying Thanksgiving together with family and loved ones.

It was a bit hard to think of bundling up Mom to travel to Aunt Maxine's house for Thanksgiving, so they all volunteered to come over to our house and make it work. Grandpa Briggs and Aunt Phoebe walked down from their house and we played on the swings out back and it was a memorable day. Jimmy was my favorite cousin and he was a bit of a prankster. He took great pride in teasing my sister every chance he got.

Later in the morning, Mom and Dad shooed us out of the house to go play in the snow. We bundled up and ventured out into six or eight inches of new and heavy snow. Looking over on the hill that was Center Street above 600 east, we were happy to see that it was still snow-covered. That meant spectacular sledding.

We had the best wooden sleds with iron rails that money could buy and we used them most of the winter sledding down Center Street over by Grandpa's house. We could coast all the way to our house once the track had turned a bit packed and icy. Few cars ventured up Center Street on a snowy morning and more often than not, they would slide off into the curb before getting up that hill. Great fun to watch!

Dale was generally a bit more fearless and took more chances than the other brothers. Alan didn't really try the slopes much and Grant and I preferred to take things at a more leisurely pace even though we could be really competitive. Dale preferred to go full out and pretty soon he was in competition with Jimmy to see who could sail the fastest and farthest on their sleds. They got running faster and longer distances before they planted their sleds and jumped on racing to see who would go fastest and farthest. It was a good thing that they knew how to steer those things. Tubing was never as fun and neither were those saucers because they couldn't be controlled.

Jimmy was a full year older and a bit heavier than Dale and on that last race, it was an all-out heated competition and by my estimation, Jimmy won. Dale whined about something being unfair and Jimmy wasn't going to take much of that for very long. It could have gotten to mittened fists, but snowballs were better. In the spirit of the challenge, we divided up and allowed fifteen minutes for each team to build a fort and then the battle would be on. Dale and I teamed up while Jimmy and Grant went to build their fort. The goal was to capture the other guy's fort and there had to be a sound strategy involved, not just pelting each other with snowy iceballs.

Snow forts had to be thick structures to withstand the onslaught and possible assault. They had to be three feet high to provide a degree of cover from getting hit. It would never be enough for competing teams to just sit behind their forts and lob heavy snowballs at the other fort. That could go on for hours and produce little. Sneak attacks and flanking maneuvers were common and once in a while if there were enough guys, a full frontal assault could pay off.

Fearless Dale saw a potential weakness to their fort location and he explained how his flanking attack would cause havoc. Jimmy and Grant had built their fort relatively close to the front porch thinking that they would have coverage and protection from a three-foot high porch on their side. That would only leave the street side and front exposed, unless someone was dumb enough to try a rear assault by going clear around the house. That would be dumb because it would be noticed and that would leave their fort only protected by one person who couldn't take out two attackers in frontal assault.

So you see, there is a bit of strategy to be evaluated and exploited and fort placement was important. Our fort was located with the aim to cancel out flanking attacks. There were trees there. There was also the other corner of the house and porch. Our plan involved a bit of luck mixed with a bit of danger for Dale. He had to get on the porch unseen and crawl on his belly across the porch unnoticed. Then he would have to climb and launch himself down on the enemy from the porch railing and wipe out their fort.

We had lobbed a few balls at the opponent and they had answered with a few of their own. Get a pattern going, we both knew how to play this. Our challenge was to ultimately line our fort's wall with as many usable snowballs so we could rise and throw them as fast as possible to keep their heads down behind their fort while Dale hopped the railing and got on the porch unseen.

At the silent signal, we both rose and each threw a couple of fast and hard snowballs at Jimmy and Grant. They ducked down while I grabbed those on my wall and threw them as fast as I could while Dale vaulted over the railing and onto the porch and lay flat. I fell down behind the wall and waited for them to reply with a hail of balls, which they did. It felt like they were going to pelt the walls of my fort until it gave in, but in reality they were only adding to our fort with more ice and snow. I lobbed a few more out there and tried to make it appear that Dale was with me and I rose my voice and told Dale to aim for their right side. Of course that was a rouse to make them think that Dale was still with me.

It took a while for Dale to inch across the porch and I was wondering what Jimmy and Grant were plotting. They weren't that dumb to just wait it out and freeze in their fort. They were evaluating options and knowing Jimmy, it probably would be pretty fearsome. He could throw his bulk at our walls and decimate us. I risked a peak over the wall to see where they were and I tossed off a couple of fastballs at them. I seemed to be a little focused on hitting their right side and whoever was there. They seemed to be focused on that as well.

For a couple of minutes I thought they had come up with a plan. They started launching some high balls into the trees and knocking off some heavy limbs of snow down onto me. That wasn't pleasant and they thought they had come up with something which would persuade me to leave my fort and attack them. I wasn't going to fall for that even though it was annoying and their little cat calls were only taunts to make be mad. I wished Dale would hurry up. He should be in position any time now.

As if on cue, there was a bloodcurdling scream and I looked up for a second to see Dale launch himself into space from the porch railing near their fort. It was amazing to witness. He landed hard on their fort and fell inward on the two boys. He kicked and waved his arms like a madman and practically leveled their fort. I jumped up, ran across, and completed the frontal assault and we took their position winning the game. Victory felt so sublime.

Luckily, before a fight could ensue, we were called in to get ready for Thanksgiving meal and we felt all the more proud because of our accomplishment. The meal itself is hard to remember except that it was probably turkey, but the victory would be savored much longer.

In the afternoon before dessert, we played Monopoly and Clue. I couldn't even get hotels up before Dale just plowed everyone into bankruptcy. There was always ample holiday music on the stereo console in the television cabinet and later tonight there was a special featured show of the Mitch Miller Sing-Along and I'm sure Mom would love that. Music has a way of lifting spirits.

After the sing-along with Mitch, Mom got this idea that she would like to have her family sing a song that we had performed a couple of years ago in church. We had been asked to sing "Sweet Hour of Prayer" on page 166 in the hymnbook. I remember the many days spent as a family practicing and learning that song. I will never forget the words to it. It would practically become our family hymn because we all knew it backwards and forwards.

It had a special meaning and melancholy on this Thanksgiving. It was our realization that we wouldn't be singing this song with Mom anymore. These next months would give new and heartfelt meaning to the word in the song "in seasons of distress and grief" and little did we know how many prayers would be launched at the heavens in the coming months. Here are the words of that song that was our family's song.

This would be the last time we would sing it as a complete family, but this evening was not over yet. It was going to get harder still.

Sweet Hour of prayer, sweet hour of prayer!
That calls me from a world of care,
And bids me at my Father's throne
Make all my wants and wishes known.
In seasons of distress and grief,
My soul has often found relief
And oft escaped the tempter's snare
By thy return, sweet hour of prayer!
Sweet hour of prayer, Sweet hour of prayer!
Thy wings shall thy petition bear
To Him whose truth and faithfulness
Engage the waiting soul to bless.
And since He bids me seek His face,
Believe His word and trust His grace.
I'll cast on Him my every care,
And wait for thee, sweet hour of prayer.

CHAPTER 6

November 23, 1967
Bountiful, Utah

The song ended and with it descended a deep sadness that was palpable. That was probably not the way that Mom intended it. Those were happy times when we sang that song. She wanted to revive that family spirit and boy did it backfire. I know that she felt it too and she asked Dad to wheel her back to her room.

It was dessert time when Aunt Maxine made an attempt to lift spirits. She felt it too, but just allowed Dad to take care of Mom. There were more dessert delicacies at Thanksgiving time than we could ever eat and I was determined to try everything—except for Aunt Maxine's mince pie. To be honest, we all made an attempt to be a bit jovial, but it wasn't working. Sure I loaded my plate and went to sit down in the living room where the grownups would sit. Dad and Mom were not there and as I tried to eat my apple pie, I found that there was a lump in my throat that wouldn't let me swallow very well.

I thought back to a movie we had seen earlier this year. It was called *Follow Me Boys* and Fred McMurray (Lem Siddons) was spectacular in leading boys as well as his family. They built their dream as a family and as boy scouts. They had a neat family and they had some tough times, but they always came out ahead and everyone in town loved them and gave him a parade. Why were we stuck "in seasons of distress and grief?"

Later we would look back on this particular Thanksgiving of 1967 as the Thanksgiving Confession. That's a dumb way to remember a special time of giving thanks and expressing gratitude. Expressing gratitude is healing and healthy. It makes room to turn over a new leaf and make additional blessings flow. For this one Thanksgiving, different from all others past or future, the rule was broken and it became "Thanksgiving Confession."

Back in Mom and Dad's room, a different conversation was going on. We knew what Dad's frame of mind was and we just caught a glimpse of Mom's before she was wheeled out. You know, we weren't dumb kids, but their privacy was important for Mom's sake. Here's the conversation. Mom was a bit awed by the song. She knew that this was the last time we would sing that and that fact brought no peace.

"Basil, Christmas is shortly upon us. If it comes, it will depend upon you to bring it. We have sheltered our kids from this disease and the knowledge of my true condition and we will need to get through one more Christmas. I want your promise that you will make it happen. I have nothing left inside to give to make it so except for the desire to see my last Christmas with my family around me as it used to be. Yesterday, I reviewed all of the Christmas cards we sent with the pictures of the children. They are so precious. There's the one with all of them in the bathtub. I'll bet in forty years they will think they were so corny. Then there's this one where they each had a silvery bell with their head photograph pasted to the bell. I've been thinking of silver bells lately. The years of Christmas have been good to us. The memories are imprinted for life and they must and will be treasured happy moments.

"This year, all I ask for myself is for peace of mind and spirit to endure what I must. But my request to you is to complete this memory for my children. There is a song that has come to some popularity these last couple of years. We learned it in *Sweet Adelines*. It is called "Silver Bells." There is a little narrative right before the music starts that many have forgotten is really part of the song. That last part of the narrative is 'whatever happens or what may be here is what Christmas means to me.' Then the music continues and 'children laughing, people passing, meeting smile after smile.' Keep it together for this year and I'll be with you each year thereafter."

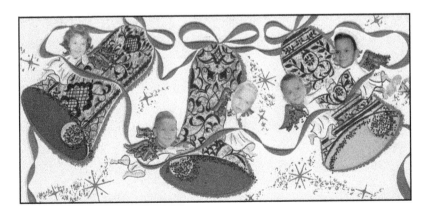

"Honey, I will do all that I can." I'm sure that Dad was caught without words of encouragement and cheer, but he forced some out anyway:

"Please don't think so low. I'm sure you'll be the light of this year's Christmas as you have been the inspiration for so many others."

"No, I'm afraid not. The light is hurt. It burns low and dim. I can't even be a beacon to myself through all of this. Pray for me to find peace with what must come, because I truly see no peace in it. God grant me to see His purpose in all this when sometimes the bitter taste is all there is. I always thought I would be around to raise these promised children. What peace or purpose is there in depriving me of this? And this is Christmas time when we enjoy each other more than any other time. Yet I look into the eyes of my children, eyes brimming with shiny anticipation and confidence, and I have none. I see no justice; I pray for mercy, I'm granted no answer. But their eager faces and smiles cut me up inside because I long and love to be their mother. Yet it is not to be. Why?"

Dad's reply was delivered slowly and with no small amount of pleading. "Please don't go on. It'll be all right. Tomorrow will be better. Maybe we should go to the mall in Salt Lake and see Santa arrive. That has always brightened your spirits. How about we go out and get some mince pie and watch some Lawrence Welk?"

With that reply, the confession was over but not the weight. Something had just gone out of Dad. That's the weight of heavy wet snow on pines. Limbs bent and ready to snap. But this is the season to be jolly and he would bring that through to us; but would Mom be granted her Christmas wish for a bit of peace? "Ring a ling, hear them ring. Soon it will be Christmas Day."

True to form back in the living room, Lawrence Welk had a Thanksgiving special edition of his show. We were all in rapt attention (or at least faking it.) Lawrence Welk was not cool! The Monkees were cool. But I endured Lawrence to keep the grownups happy and think that I was getting culture.

Mom came out for the last half of the show and she seemed to feel relieved. She loved Lawrence Welk's musical numbers and the dancing. There would be no dancing, but she could watch and join in the spirit of that blended with a bit of mince pie. I had no idea how she could eat that, but she did.

We closed off the evening in family prayer. It was rare for us to hear Grandpa Briggs give the prayer and it was wonderful. Despite his sometimes gruff exterior, he was a deep-feeling father and he had seen his share of adversity. He would be a strength to his family throughout whatever was to come and he prayed that the angels would attend to his family in this special and hallowed season.

We all went to our beds that night with a little more knowledge and a little more reality. We were accustomed to kneel beside our beds and "pray out" in the evening and that night I did "cast on Him my every care." I just hope I could recognize the answer when it came.

CHAPTER 7

December 4, 1967
Bountiful, Utah

Monday night was this thing that was called "Family Home Evening." Sort of a new concept, but we embraced it. As a family, we spent a lot of time together; practically every evening was a family home evening, but here was a church-mandated opportunity, so why not? It was also fully into Christmas time!

Christmas, the old ones say, reeks nostalgia, anticipation, and hope. Mom always said so too, so it must be true. Though dull within her own spirit, she lived this season through the eyes of her children. I think that this season was the only thing that got her through despair and despondency that she must be feeling. I could tell and Dad could tell. Dad's twenty-one and three quarters years married to a woman gives a certain degree of discernment. In spite of it all, Mom was superconfident with her children.

She got us excited to write our letters to Santa Claus, correcting the spelling of such difficult words as telescope, recorders, and bicycles. Somehow she seemed to leave us with assurance that each and every letter would receive due consideration by the jolly old elf.

Today we were going out to select the all-important Christmas tree. That required special consideration in the tree lots downtown. Mom deemed it wise not to come, but assured us that hot chocolate and postum would be waiting when we arrived home. Alan chose to stay and keep her company, maybe help get things off the high kitchen shelves.

The choice between Christmas trees was no easy matter. Did we want the bushy tree or the one that had a more spindly look to it with branches protruding in several directions, all outward from the trunk? Some say there is a symbolism in Christmas trees. I thought it was bunk and amounted to personal preference. I spent more time wandering the lot, leaving the hard work and choice up to others who knew the rules of tree-choosing.

As soon as it was selected, Dad always requested that they hack off a couple of inches on the base. I thought it was because he knew precisely the height that would fit in our house including the angel on top. It could be that there was another reason. It didn't matter though. We arrived home and dragged that thing up the stairs and into the house and miraculously, it was just right when we stood it up. Dads are pretty clever, aren't they?

Mom made her way into the living room and Alan followed with the warm drinks. I used to love Postum more than hot chocolate and that was my warm beverage of choice. It had to have plenty of sugar, though, or else it was pretty bitter and then just the right amount of cream or milk.

The decorating would be supervised by the mother in the home. Dads didn't have the eye for that, so Dad just sat back and watched as Mom directed the decorating. She was always big on the red glass ornaments, and they had to be placed in just the right proportions of the three sizes and in strategically defined places all over the tree. She also was partial to red lights on the trees. We also had these medium-sized bulbs that always seemed a bit much for a tree, but it would be beautiful. This year Mom chose to have us thread popcorn and let that be the garland for the tree.

We rarely went for a flocked tree at Christmas. Mom didn't like the mess and always felt that snow belonged outside. A green and fragrant tree was her idea of Christmas. Men had no eye for decorating a tree. They had no artistic mind and I soon learned that my part of decorating was to make sure that Ellen didn't eat any of those smaller red balls. Not only would that throw off the artistry and count, but Ellen might have some adverse tummy effects.

We had a few special ornaments that seemed to go up every year and then there would be a couple of special additions later when we added the ones that we made in school. The final act was for Dad to place the Christmas angel ornament on top of the tree. Then Alan had the honor of lighting the tree.

We passed out this thin book of Christmas carols and sang a bunch of Christmas songs and then we were told to finish off our lists and get them turned in so they could get mailed tomorrow. "The spelling better be right too," was the warning.

The last thing that came out of the decorations box was an old porcelain nativity set. It was special because it reminded us of the simple meaning that kept escaping us this year. There was a babe that was born in a faraway world and this baby was born to die. There was a price required at the time of His birth. That price would be a life and we all sang for joy because of this event.

I took special care in writing my list. It was a long list. I knew that we could do it because Dad had finally sold the house that we had built. He was happy that he had a fair price for it. He even gave me and the other boys $100 dollars that we could spend, although Mom urged us to put it into the bank and save it. We would never know when we might need it. I followed that advice, but I knew that potentially we could have a pretty fine Christmas.

We turned in our lists just before we went to bed, satisfied that this was going to happen. Gifts are gifts; little did we realize that there was a price attached at the time. After all, Santa would make it happen and he had unlimited resources. The concept of a price tag attached to gifts was only for stores or malls where people bought things for each other. Dad announced that on Saturday we would be making a trip into Salt Lake to see Santa at the Cottonwood Mall. That was always a neat event.

I was a bit mature for my age and I would be twelve this month. I didn't realize (in spite of my maturity) that what I was thinking was really in conflict, but that's the nature of the twelve-year-old mind. At the time that I was thinking that we would have a great Christmas because Dad sold the house (and therefore had money), it didn't equate with the idea that Santa could get us anything regardless of cost or money.

My supposed "higher maturity" was trying to reach beyond the Santa concept and teach me that there is a price required for things that we value. Even a price was required of a perfect being who was born to pay the price of something that I couldn't quite fathom, but there was a notion blossoming in this semimature brain that even heaven-sent gifts have a price required.

I'm sure Mom and Dad knew a little about that as they met later in the evening and reviewed our lists. I'll bet they called in "Gift Gluttony" evening and now they had to sit down and review our lists. There was a process that was involved before the lists got passed on to Santa. It's called "making the cut" if something finally was considered "sent on to Santa."

In the first round of "cuts," it was relatively easy to axe out Dale's dirt bike. (He already had a good bike.) Grant's new rocking chair fell as well in the first round as did my .22 rifle, Alan's TV set, and Ellen's live puppy dog. The second round of cuts were a little harder, but once accomplished, there was a working list for "Santa" to use when he visited the mall and could see in person whether we were naughty or nice.

CHAPTER 8

December 9, 1967
Cottonwood Mall, Salt Lake City, Utah

Going to the Cottonwood Mall was a treat at Christmastime. We never had to be outside in the cold and there seemed to be a hundred stores under a roof. There was a big common area and the magic of Christmas was everywhere. Right in the middle Santa has built a house and had a few elves helping with the crowds.

It was amazing! There was everything right there. I spent a lot of time in Woolworth's and the Skaggs store because they had the most toys. Dad couldn't be there with everyone and Mom had elected not to challenge the crowds at this place. They were also huge and a little annoying. Dad split us up into groups of three. I went with Alan and Ellen. Dad had Dale and Grant and then we would meet and switch off.

We simply could not miss our visit with Santa and hopefully Dad had brought our lists so he could deliver them in person or put them in the little box for mail near his house. I knew that Dad wouldn't forget something so important.

We got a little tired and needed a change of pace after Woolworth's, so we headed over to the line to visit Santa. Boy, was it long! We would probably be there at least an hour in kid time and that was longer than adult time. Those kids up there must have massive lists of presents and things to tell Santa. I just knew that if I had to wait an hour in line, I would probably pee my pants.

While we were waiting, I got to talking to Ellen mostly and to Alan a little bit. We wondered what we might get for Christmas this year. I had a bit of a preoccupation with whether I was on the nice list. As I had counted my deeds, I got to thinking that it could go either way. I mentioned my concern to my brother and sister. They were pretty much quiet on the subject, not wanting to cast a vote or perhaps they had other plans that I didn't know about. That thought had me a little worried.

I fidgeted and stewed in that line and the more I fidgeted, the more I contemplated my misdeeds that year. Guilt sort of has a taxing effect, especially when it meant more toys or no toys. I rationalized that I was almost twelve now and toys shouldn't be my main preoccupation. That was my "semimature" side fighting with my kid side. After all, I should be a little concerned about what to get Mom for Christmas and stop thinking about myself.

Twelve-year-olds have these constant battles between kid maturity and higher-level maturity. This was not a good time for me to have this battle. Long lines allow for too much thinking. In my paranoia, I started to fixate on one scary possibility: it was entirely possible that Alan or Ellen were going to rat me out when they got to Santa's lap. It was conceivable that Santa might ask them if they had a good brother named David. They could sell me out!

I glanced over at Alan and he gave me that older brother look like he had something on me. Ellen was at my side and she was looking all innocent and seven years old little princess. I started to wonder how they would sell me out, that spoiled little sister with the innocent look! I could have been nicer, but now is not the time while waiting to see Santa. I bent over so that I could whisper to her and look her right in those baby blue eyes.

"Ellen, have you thought of what you want to tell Santa…err…I mean ask him for Christmas?" I spoke in most sweetest tones.

"Oh sure, I want a really neat dolly that laughs and cries and pees."

"So, Sis, if Santa asks something else. . . . Let's say about your favorite and cool brother, what would you say?"

"Oh, that's easy: I tell them that Alan is the most kind and cool brother and he deserves to get a television if one can fit in the sleigh."

Oh, brother. My sister is an airhead. She doesn't even realize that I am the cool brother! But let's keep this bright and cheery and not plant thoughts in her head.

"Sis, you are so observant. Alan is a cool brother and you only have cool brothers. How about we make a little deal here just for the brothers' sake and we'll back you up and do the same for you? What do you say to only telling Santa how great your brothers are and leave out any other indiscretions that might pop into your mind?"

"What's an indegretion, David?"

Ooops, I forgot I'm older and I use bigger words than she does. What would she understand? I got it!

"It means that there is no tattling on any of us to Santa. We're just the best brothers that you could hope for. Can you do that if he asks about us?"

"Oh sure, David. I couldn't fink on my brothers to Santa." Ellen gave me that little cutsie look with a wink so I couldn't tell if she was telling the truth, but I had played my cards and I wasn't going to beat this one. It will be what it will be. In another fifteen minutes, our chat would be over and I could go find Dad and switch out this little rat-fink.

By the time we got to Santa, I was fairly doing a little nervous dance. It was not so much that I was worried about this visit, but I really had to go pee. It was great to sit on his lap, although he commented that I was no small fry any longer. I guess my time of lap-sitting had passed. I was getting older and more mature after all.

We finished and got our candy canes from the elf then went looking for Dad. We found him waiting in line with Dale and Grant. Now was not the time to switch out unless Alan wanted to wait with them and let Dad go with us. Alan gave me that look again as I set off with Dad to find a bathroom. I had no idea if Alan would squeal on me to Santa, but I decided he was better than that.

Dad took us back through some of the same stores and a few others. I think (in my mature-self-way) that he was checking to see what would light up our eyes. Probably so he could tell Santa. I was looking hard at this telescope. I loved looking up at the stars. But I was also torn because a cool guy would want a recorder or a nice record player to play cool songs on. I was starting to collect a few "45's" and this would help establish my 'coolness' after sixth grade when I switched over to junior high school.

I asked Dad what Mom would like for Christmas. The usual reply was "Just you smiling." He said that every year, but I felt that she needed something special this year. He looked me in the eye with that tired Dad look and said, "Son, could you pray that she gets what *she* really wants for Christmas?"

"I suppose I could do that, but it might help if you gave me a clue."

"Oh, you'll know. I hear that in other countries, some children ask

Baby Jesus for gifts. I think it would be well to ask Baby Jesus to give Mom the best thing in the world and that she'll know it when she gets it."

Now, I had just learned from my vocabulary list what "cryptic" meant and this qualified. I could even spell the word since I had sort of gift for seeing a word and then spelling it. I chose not to ask Dad for any clarification. We finished our shopping and on the way home Dad told us that he wanted to take a drive around Temple Square and see the lights before we went home.

Temple Square in Salt Lake was where light and hope reverberated for us. This is where dreams came true. Dad and Mom had got married right here about twenty two years ago or something like that. I know they told us the story and that this was a reverent and holy place. We didn't come here often, but the lights and the cheery sounds inside of those walls could be felt in our car as we headed home.

On the way home we sang a favorite which was "Jingle Bells." I could tell that Dad was either deep in thought or deep in prayer. I'm sure he really wanted to give Mom what she wanted most in life. She hadn't really found the peace that she wanted and he was the proof of that because he was going through the motions of her request. Yes we knew about it because little kids have feelings and half-mature kids are notorious.

I wondered on that little drive home if our prayers were holding back God's purpose. What should we be praying for? If we pray for Mom to live longer and be our mom, are we holding her in suffering mode? It's not right to pray for the opposite either. So I think that Dad was wise in asking us to ask Baby Jesus for what Mom wanted most right now, the best thing for her, whatever that might be, and that we would be able to accept that and deal with whatever that choice was.

Somewhere is all of this excitement was a true meaning of Christmas. It really wasn't in the mall lined up to sit on Santa's lap and it wasn't in trimming out a tree.

CHAPTER 9

December 16, 1967
Bountiful, Utah

Tonight was the night of our congregation's Christmas Party. What an event! All my friends would be there. Janet would be there. It was a grand opportunity to eat and goof off with the cool people. I fit right in with that.

Mom was feeling a little upbeat and wanted to go at least for a little bit she told Dad. Dad bundled her up in the wheelchair and all we had to do was walk across the street. That should be easy and Mom and Dad had a lot of friends at church. Dad had been a counselor in the bishopric for a long time and knew everyone.

It was common knowledge that Santa would make an appearance at this event, but us older and slightly mature kids knew that this Santa was a fake because the real one was still over at the mall in Salt Lake. Nevertheless we could play our part and keep spirits up and hopefully word would get back to the real Santa anyway. That's where it counted.

Of course we brought green jello with pineapple in it to this grand party. There would be plenty of green jello to have leftovers to take home. I think that was the point, right? Somewhere we could smell ham roasting and we pretty much knew what the meal would be. There was plenty of fun between food, Christmas carols, and the appearance of the fake

Santa.…Whoops…I mean just plain Santa to keep spirits high and not slowing down.

Mom left for home with Dad after a short time, but she had appeared happy and genuinely glad to see her friends and loved ones. We didn't realize it, but this would be her last appearance at a ward party. It's sort of like everything was being her last and that thought didn't settle in with us until February.

Sure I got asked lots of questions by my friends. Janet even asked me about my mom. I told her that she was sick with something called cancer and her body was fighting it. That seemed to appease kids because they had no idea of a killer when they saw one. I didn't want to bash in their dreams and I sure didn't want a pity party and a boo-hoo fest. That was not cool!

At 9:00 p.m., Dad sent Alan over to tell us to come home. It was time for bed. We told our friends good-bye and made a couple of plans for Monday in school. Santa had been great and we didn't tease or tug at his beard. We were a support, if you can believe that!

Back at home it was prayer time and Mom said the prayer from her seat while we kneeled around. I was especially interested in what she would pray for since it would give a clue to what she really wanted. True to form, she got right into it and prayed that our Christmas season would make a marvelous memory. She prayed that we would remain together, strong, and united in this troubling world. She prayed for the sick and afflicted to be healed. I have to admit that I opened my eyes on that one and looked at her. This was a standard request in prayer, but did she mean it? I felt at the time that these were just words and they didn't penetrate the ceiling because she didn't really believe them. That was sad, but then she got serious. She asked to have the strength to see Father's will in her life and accept it, that it was His will that counted and she had felt unworthy to know it. She wanted to know it now. I peeked again and that one went home, far beyond the ceiling of our house on Center Street.

She closed the prayer a few moments later, but I still didn't really know what that meant. It was still a bit cryptic (as I understood the word to mean) and I went to bed wondering. This was Saturday night and it was close to Christmas, so in keeping with a long standing custom, Dale, Grant, and I sat in the family room downstairs to talk. We had some thoughts about Christmas this year as compared with other years. Something just wasn't the same as other years.

We talked about that memorable Christmas a couple of years ago when I got to catch Santa in the act. They wanted me to tell the story again so I did. I wouldn't ever forget it.

Christmas Eve 1965 was like any other Christmas Eve at our home and I suppose that in retelling the story, it helps to understand why this Christmas might be a little different. Dad would read to us from the Bible about the Christmas Story and we would listen to a tape recording of the "Journey to Bethany" which was a story about the coming of Christ. We all listened with the attention level required of Christmas Eve and the anticipation of tomorrow's presents.

After the stories, we had family prayer and then Dad took a few moments to warn us not to be up and about before 7:00 a.m. and that there would be traps for any who thought the rule didn't apply to them. If any person was caught, that would be the end of his presents. Odd that he directed his speech directly at the boys. Ellen would never dream of breaking the 7:00 a.m. rule and risking the loss of presents.

We all went downstairs and had a prearranged time when we would meet in the family room. Alan was not a conspirator and promptly went to bed or to read. We settled in our beds for about an hour that seemed to stretch on forever and always ran the risk of falling asleep. On this one night of nights, there was little chance of nodding off. The excitement level was way too high.

At around 11:00 p.m., we silently gathered in the darkness of the family room. We were not about to risk any lighting that would give us away and we were silent as ghosts. We sat there on the couch in the family room and just listened. The family room was directly below the living room. We even had a fireplace in the basement which was in the same position as the fireplace above. Anyone attempting entry through the chimney would be heard.

I'll bet that Grant was experiencing some mighty urges to start "bumping" on the couch. This physical activity must have been a powerful stress reducer for him because he could just slam himself forward and back against the couch for hours. We called it "bumping," but it was therapy for him and he had to resist the impulse there as we waited in silence to hear if anything was going on upstairs.

We half expected Dad to come checking on the kids at any time, so we kept one ear listening for the stairs to creak. Dad could show up at any time and the whole deal would be over plus Christmas presents. We risked everything just for the thrill of it. That's how it was in 1965 and it was the beginning of my "coolness."

After about an hour we felt that there was something going on upstairs. It was so faint but once in a while there would be a creak distinguished above the other normal sounds of a house and fireplace cooling down for the night. We looked at each other and sort of knew that the time had arrived. I crawled over to the fireplace to listen better and I could swear that something was happening. Perhaps it was more of a feeling rather than actual disturbed sound waves.

Excitement turned up a notch as I returned to the couch to report. This was the real deal and we needed to check it out. Dale warned against any action that would cost us our loot at this early stage. Our whispered debate was earnest, yet really quiet. My argument was that this was our chance. No one has ever caught Santa in the act! And Dale's reply was equally succinct in that no one ever wanted to risk losing all the presents either.

Sitting there waiting was really more than I could handle as a new ten-year-old. I had to act. I told them that I was going to check it out since they were scaredy-cats. Dale just looked at me and shrugged as if to say, *It's your funeral, Bro.* Grant was excited for me and agreed to go with me over to the stairs.

The stairs were going to be treacherous. Dad always had traps on the stairs since he was a devious man. The stairs also creaked and you had to know just how to move to not make a sound. The first few steps were easy. Just stay to the outside as you crawled upward. There was no creaking if you were against the side walls. We had learned that from other Christmas practice runs.

The first sign of traps was the rice krispies on the steps. This was a minor nuisance and easily brushed to the center so I could continue going up. The next trap was discovered with bells stretched across the stairs tied to the railing and taped on the opposite wall. I found them by carefully and oh so slowly running my hand on the railing and finding a string tied there. You didn't want to dismantle this trap because it would make a noise and noise was the enemy. My solution was to stay close to the railing wall and crawl at a level below the railing and get past this one.

Immediately after clearing the bell trap, I felt the "stack" trap. This is where the pots and pans were all stacked precariously on a step so that at the slightest vibration or touch, everything would come crashing down and the whole house would be instantly awake. This was a bad one and I could have easily toppled the whole mess. Luckily I had felt a pan from the bottom and just glazed it enough to know what it was.

Knowing the trap was only the first and easiest part of solving it. I couldn't simply bypass this one. It had to be removed at the risk of toppling everything and I couldn't even see where to begin and touching was treacherous. This trap called for extreme risk and I could tell that Grant was waiting there at the bottom of the stairs and wondering why it took so long. I really only had one choice in this darkness and that choice was to risk a flash of dim light.

I had a small flashlight for just such an emergency. I had to see what I was dealing with, but I could only risk a short burst of a faint light. I put my hand over the lens as I rested beneath the treacherous bell trap. I turned on the light, which might have caused Grant a little concern. I saw my hand glow reddish with the light on, but that wasn't enough. I risked a partially covered and controlled burst of light right at the problem area.

As it briefly flashed over the trap, I saw the order of this mess and how to overcome it. Now I knew where the top was and that if I started at the top and carefully removed a pan at a time, I could put them on the far side in a stable and noiseless stack. Carefully and quietly I started at the top and placed each pan out of harm's way. I didn't need the light to do it because in that one burst of light, the placement was memorized and the solution was clear.

After I had moved them, I paused to breathe and listen to see if I had aroused anyone by the brief use of light. All was silent and I felt safe enough to proceed. More rice krispies but no more serious traps. In turning to the left and going into the kitchen, there were more messes on the floor and a few scattered spoons and forks. Not even a challenge, but the real challenge was not to move where a creak would be made.

My theory in dealing with this problem of the creak was to lay my body flat out and distribute the weight over a broader area so that the floor wouldn't sense a weight issue and creak. The theory proved to be sound and in this case I was able to proceed soundlessly lying flat on my stomach and pulling myself across the linoleum as I scooted the obstacles to the side. Once I made it to the dining room, things would get interesting since the dining room was open to the living room and that's what I wanted to see.

As I neared the dining room entrance, I decided that I was just going to be taking a quick peek. There was light in the living room. The red Christmas tree lights were still on and there were a few coals in the fireplace. Not much light, but enough to get a quick glimpse and memorize the layout just like I had done with the pan trap.

I was down low to the floor. In an instant, I pulled myself into view of the living room, looked, and pushed back again out of sight. The brief glimpse would be forever locked in my memory. I had been blessed with a memory like that. It wasn't photographic or anything quite that grand, but I could see a word, for example, and then I could spell it easily. My mind just trapped things and held them and this picture would always be there.

I saw a larger person in the living room between the tree and the fireplace so it was mostly in red light and in shadow, but it was a person. He was doing something, but I couldn't tell in that brief glimpse what he was doing. I knew that it wasn't my dad because this guy was a little bigger and bulkier. There were presents all over the place, some piles larger than others. The work was still underway and I had seen it!

One of my toughest decisions as a newly minted ten-year-old cool kid was whether I should risk another look, perhaps a little longer glance to confirm. I lay there debating with myself. I had thus far been undetected and I had made it all the way to see what I saw. I could quit while I was ahead, but I also desperately wanted to confirm what I had seen and log another snapshot in my brain. I agonized for about three minutes hardly taking a breath.

In the end, the safe side won. Dale's words downstairs about risking it all were too much and I had glimpsed what "all" was there in the living room. I didn't like my chances. I had been good and lucky so far.

I suppose that if it had been Dale who did take chances, he would have risked another look. I had accomplished what I had intended and few others could claim what I could claim. I had seen him and I was, no doubt, the coolest kid in history.

I never was caught. I made it back downstairs and my story was so cool that Dale was convinced to make a try. I had paved the way and he had an easy run that year. But by the time Dale got there, our visitor was gone and Dale actually went into the living room and pawed through presents and saw what each person was going to get.

So here we are in 1967 and reliving the Christmas when I caught Santa. This year wasn't quite the same and we could feel that it was a bit difference. We really couldn't come up with a plan for this year. We talked a little, but a scheme just didn't seem to resonate. Maybe we were thinking about Mom's prayer and wondering. We would get together another day and hopefully figure things out.

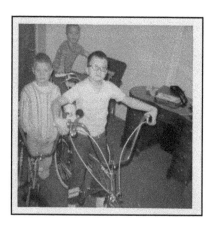

Christmas 1965

CHAPTER 10

December 23, 1967
Bountiful, Utah

It's my birthday!! I was twelve years old and I had achieved "coolness." This was an impressive accomplishment. I also got to share the birthday with Joseph Smith and my parents had almost named me Joseph, but I suppose there were a lot of Joseph Asays and they settled on David after the president of the church at the time.

Mom and Dad did their best to make my birthday a celebration, but it was so close to Christmas that it seemed that Christmas seemed to eclipse the birthday anyway. We had cake and presents at around 5:00 p.m. in the afternoon, but the real plan was to go to the annual Christmas pageant in the old Bountiful Tabernacle.

Earlier this morning, Mom had announced that we seem to be missing the real spirit of Christmas and we needed to get it back on track. She realized it was my birthday and didn't want to take away from that, but she wanted us to attend the pageant as a family and get some religion in and remember that it is Jesus we are celebrating and that there is Christ in Christmas.

So her announcement was a bit cliché and we knew that, but did this mean that Mom was going to go and be with us? Did she have the strength to be there? Would she be a spectacle for others to gawk at? This was the most positive endeavor she had made so far and this was wonderful. I could tell that Dad was excited at the prospect and that maybe her mood was improving. She really wanted to do this with her children so that we all knew that she was getting into this true meaning of Christmas.

The pageant started at 7:00 p.m., so it was good that we had got my birthday celebration out of the way. It was a little cloudy outside and could snow sometime later, but the temperature wasn't terribly cold thanks to the cloud cover I suppose. We all got bundled up and even donned knitted scarves and Mom was wheeled out and then lifted into our little Ford station wagon. She seemed so small and fragile as Dad lifted her into the seat.

It would be a short five-block drive to the tabernacle down on Main Street. Bountiful City workers and the store owners on Main Street always went overboard on Christmas decorations and it was incredible to look down the street at the holiday transformation. We didn't pause to admire this since it was a priority to get Mom inside the building and find a good place to sit.

Every Christmas pageant seems to have some common elements like a stable and livestock of some sort. There would be shepherds, wisemen, and a manger. Those are the basic elements together with a Mary and Joseph and a baby. We knew the story, but it was really cool to be experiencing it with Mom since she hadn't been present for most of our Christmas events. It made it all feel like old times.

This year's theme was a bit different. Each time I see the Christmas story, it seems like there is a peculiar emphasis on one aspect or another and that gives added meaning to the story and also helps to hold the interest of a twelve-year-old. As the program continued, there was a narrator who told of a special event that was foretold to happen in obscure Bethlehem. As the narrator would talk, the usual people would enter the stable scene. There would be songs like *"Away in a Manger"* and *"Hark the Herald Angels Sing."*

My mom loved the music and the songs of this season and she hummed along as the program proceeded. The focus of the message the narrator delivered was on these angels who were all so excited. They were the ones who couldn't contain themselves and told the shepherds about this memorable birth. The angels were heard singing in the heavens and it was a busy night for angels. They were excited!

But just who were these beings and what could angels be? Angels came from heavenly realms and this was a spectacular event in the history of this world. This singular event and birth was the one on which everything was hinged. These angels seemed to have more than a vested interest in what was happening. We had a vested interest as children of a Heavenly Father. What if we were also there in those heavenly choirs with a real understanding of what was happening? How exciting would that be!!

I could tell that mom was soaking this in, but there was something else going on. She turned over to Dad and whispered something to him. Dad looked over at me and mouthed the words that he was going to take Mom outside for some air. Alan and I would watch the programs and take care of the smaller ones. I felt pretty big for my twelve years. Dad hadn't asked me to do that before. As he wheeled her down the aisle, I couldn't help but thinking that Mom was probably a little overloaded and self-conscious being in crowds closed in by people now.

The narrator continued to go on about the angels understanding what this night meant and that their songs were songs of something called "redeeming love." I wondered what that meant and how an act of love could have redeeming qualities. That's pretty deep, but there was also this weird thing apparently called a song of redeeming love. Angels sang it, we sang it. What was that about?! I guess someday I would have to make a point of understanding the references to a "song of redeeming love" and trying to grasp whatever that meant about a baby being born to die and that we all got excited about that. I wondered how a heavenly father felt about that program.

My mind got a little carried away into some strange thoughts as I felt things deep inside. There was a lot of mention about "joy" and "peace" in Christmas songs. I remember that Mom wanted peace and something special to give her strength for the Father's will to be done. Peace seemed to be paired with joy a lot, but I didn't see how peace would bring much joy to my mother. It might just bring an acceptance, but what would bring joy?

Outside it appeared that snow was going to be coming soon. Mom wanted to be wheeled down the sidewalk towards Main Street so that she could look at the lights and decorations. Dad could tell that her emotions were running high and he didn't need to say anything. The pageant had been just what she needed and now she needed some space. The streets were still and quiet. No one else was outside, alone in a white world just before a snowfall.

Yesterday's snow still covered the evergreens and grounds of the tabernacle. This made the Christmas lighting all the more spectacular in the stillness. Quietly Mom's words rose from her as she began to talk to her Heavenly Father. The words held all the emotion and yearning from a mother who wanted to understand. She let out all of the pain, the anxiety, the fear, and asked that her faith might bring answers. Quietly and emotionally she pleaded as if she were a young girl talking to her dad and trying to understand why boo-boos happen.

This was a season for honoring a special birth of God's Son. It was a hallowed and sacred time. Angels sang with unrestrained joy and there were their words of "Peace on Earth, Good Will toward Men." Where was that amid this fear and anxiety? Mom started to quietly sob as she spoke words that choked with emotion: "I was born to be a mother. It's all I ever wanted or dreamed of. You gave me that blessing after many years of pleading. Now it's to be ripped away by a vile disease that has ravaged me for years. I honestly don't get it. Why fulfill the promise only to painfully tear it from me?"

There was nothing Dad could do. This was literally between a daughter and her Dad. Nothing to do but be there for her if called upon. She became silent and when she looked up, tears filled her eyes and I'm sure Dad's were full as well, but words were not bidden. She looked around her. It was so still and almost surreal. Dad actually felt what was going on in his loving wife. It was as if he could feel within his body more alive than the grosser materials of a body would normally allow. Senses perked up in some unspoken anticipation of something that could never be expressed in words or emotion.

As he stood there with hands gripped on the wheelchair handles, he suddenly was not alone. Two angels appeared and took Mom in their arms and hugged her with an intensity and emotion that penetrated through to Dad as he looked on. These two angels hadn't just descended to be there. It was as if they had been there, but suddenly decided to let their presence be physically open for eyes to see and comprehend.

One of these angels was Mom's mother, my grandmother. She has passed over about ten years before and she knew firsthand of Mom's anguish over not being able to have children and then she had been there to see her daughter become a mother. The other woman was not recognized by my father, but was probably another family member or guardian angel from long ago. She looked directly into Mom's eyes with a love, compassion, and understanding that was not of this world.

Thinking about it later, Dad thought back to the pageant and thought that this woman angel could be Mary, the mother of a very special Son of God and she knew what it was like to be torn in wanting to find understanding and peace. Words were not exchanged by this angel, but the thoughts that flooded through this medium of love came in torrents. So much was laid out for her. She understood and grasped what was real and understood the meaning of it. She learned how her mission needed to be fulfilled, not just what it was but that it was clear and specific that her mission would continue and she would be a mother in Zion.

Grandma Briggs spoke few words, but left her to grasp that "the seeds of death were introduced along with the seeds of life that grew in her womb during each pregnancy." Opposites and opposition exist where great blessings abound. Although it would not really be clear to Dad, it was as if Mom had achieved a higher connection and understanding.

Fear and despair left and it was as if Mom were made whole again. When the world came back to our senses, a gentle snow was falling and the feeling and the glow remained. It was as if the embrace would remain and restore the glow and feelings that had been real. Mom would never really lose that; even as the next two months of pain might dim the body, the spirit would remain undimmed.

Dad knelt down in front of her chair and Mom and Dad looked at each other. The lights of the street were there, the light snow falling, but for a brief time, not even fifteen minutes, they knew there was a real song of redeeming love. Yes, it had been sung before. Though we don't understand many things in this Potter's body of clay, there is direction and purpose and all of us are a part of it if we would just allow it to be.

As Mom and Dad strolled back toward the tabernacle, the final verse of the closing song summarizes the feeling that had distilled upon them and they understood it firsthand. Amazingly enough it is from a song that is found just opposite the song on page 166 where we had learned "Sweet Hour of Prayer." The other song there on page 165 is called "O Little Town of Bethlehem" and its third verse rang loud in the stillness outside the tabernacle as they walked back:

"How silently, how silently; the wondrous gift is given.
So God imparts to human hearts the message of His heaven.
No ear may hear His coming, but in this world of sin,
Where meek souls will receive Him still, the dear Christ enters in."*

We joined our parents in the car for the ride home. I could tell that something had changed. Somehow inside it was clear that she had received her gift for this Christmas season. I could only equate this to a twelve-year-old looking at a Christmas morning and seeing all of that pile of toys and presents and knowing it was yours. Picture the beaming ecstasy on a child's face in that moment. That was the way I could describe Mom's look as we drove home and it made all the difference on how we would receive Christmas of 1967.

*Phillips Brooks; William Reed Huntington (ed.)

The Church Porch: A Service Book and Hymnal for Sunday Schools

(E.P. Dutton, 1882) Hymn 48

CHAPTER 11

January 6, 1968
Salt Lake City, Utah

Health issues for Mom went decidedly downhill after Christmas. By mid-morning, it was fairly evident that we were a bit out of our league even with Aunt Maxine and my cousin Judy's nursing skills. We simply didn't have the equipment or knowledge to assist with the gradual worsening of the pain.

The cancer was painfully working through the bone in her torso, but we were told that when it starts on the liver, there is a huge downturn. And after that, it would probably progress to the lungs and they would soon cease to function and breathing would be painfully shallow up until a person just drowned.

Kids didn't understand all of this and our house just had no option to keep a person comfortable and medicated through the process, so Dad and the Briggs family felt that it was best to move her to St. Mark's hospital which would be the closest facility in North Salt Lake to care for her. Preparations were made by Dr. D and at around 10:30 a.m., we followed the ambulance into the city.

Mom was conscious as they wheeled her out of her home for the last time. She knew that she was seeing it for the last time but I'm sure that she was attended by her mom and that the veil was going to be increasingly thin as the time wore on. We did get to give her a quick hug there in the living room before we piled into the car to follow. Little did I know at that last parting that I would never see her again or give her that kiss and tell her that I love her.

Upon arriving at the hospital, we were informed that anyone who was twelve and under was not allowed to go visit anyone in the hospital. No exceptions and the nurses were fairly rigorous in upholding their rule. The finality of it all didn't really dawn on me until it was far too late. I was twelve and cool and I would be graduating from primary and moving ahead into cooler things.

We were allowed to wait in the cool and antiseptic waiting room in the foyer of the hospital, but that really didn't feel right. Alan was allowed to go up to visit Mom but I could not. I think that it really hurt my mom as well to know that none of her children could come to visit. As the weeks would wear on, we, the children, would visit less and less because there was no point. The rule was the rule. We could go across the street to a park that was right near the Wasatch Hot Springs Plunge and I remember sitting there on the bench in the wintry park waiting for Dad to come and get us so we could go home, a home without a mom now.

February 19, 1968
Bountiful, UT

We had passed some dreary days of the winter under the care of Aunt Maxine. When she wasn't there, she was at the hospital. Dad would always come home late at night after spending hours in the hospital. It was draining on him. Alan would tell us a few things that were happening at the hospital. Most of February was going by and Mom didn't really know who was in the room or not. On one occasion she imagined Alan was there or some story about Alan, but she was in and out of reality and the morphine was creating hallucinations.

Early in the morning of this day, we woke up and prepared to go to school as usual. As we made our way upstairs to breakfast, there was a somber mood and we were greeted with a hug from Aunt Maxine. She informed us that Dad would be home soon and that our mother had passed away very early this morning. We probably wouldn't be going to school on this day. Grandpa Briggs would be down later and Dad would be back and we will get through this thing.

This event would prove to be life-changing for all of us. Some would heal slower than others, but there would be no forgetting this day. For this family, coming to grips with the sadness and moving forward would take a number of years.

Sometimes when you think that you have life figured out, these defining moments hit you and change your life completely. Nothing would ever be the same again. Standing in line at the viewing, five little ones listening to the whispered comments of people in the line about what a shame for these little ones. They thought we wouldn't hear. The sadness was all there was at that time.

Was God's hand there in our grief? What was God's lesson to us in this huge loss? One thing was certain: our lives would never be the same, but we could choose whether to blame the situation and wallow in it or whether we would grasp the miracle and move forward realizing that

God's love was even more outstretched. Don't tell that to a grieving child! It wouldn't go over well.

The miracle was that there were five children born to a mother who should have been barren. Five souls got to choose the life and what they would be. Some would fall victim to wallowing, hurting, and lost in relationships, even blaming the past. We would question the fairness of the whole deal. What was fair about this outcome? One defining moment, one situation of resounding loss, and it's not about fairness.

Would I change the moments that define me? Would I go back and scream "Foul!" at God for the unfairness of it all? Grief comes and there is a toll, but if you rise out of it with a deeper and more abiding love, isn't it worth it all? I ponder the grief of a mother's moments in wondering about the why in this event. Did she feel the same way about the fairness of it all? It had to be very hard, yet in our grief it's hard to see that her hurt must have been enormous.

All in all, the love of Christ must shine through as it did for her in this story. There is awe and majesty in that love and trust and the assurance that we will overcome. Healing would be different for each of us depending on whether we could convert this "fairness" argument with God into a demonstration of "love" administered by God.

Many years later, life would throw another curve ball with the death of a daughter-in-law who died leaving four little ones behind for a father to raise. Now Grandpa knows a little about their grief and when they get past the point of the "fairness" argument, he can teach them about the "love." Had he not been there, he would not really know. Life has a way of providing teaching moments if we take them into our hearts in the way they were intended by a loving God.

AFTERWORD

Though sad and deep as some losses may be and though we may perpetuate a life as a victim of such losses and never reach for understanding the cost and lesson associated, it is unfair to perpetuate the injustice of it all across generations and stain a life that could have been magnificent except for the perpetuity of remaining a victim.

There is a scripture in John 15:13: "Greater love hath no man than this, that a man lay down his life for his friends." What it means is celebrating the Christmas story or celebrating a life freely given that we might have life. That's what it literally was for the children of Wanda Briggs Asay.

The truth behind the story was that she was told by Dr. D and others that she was not going to have children. For years she wondered since it took so long for her to get pregnant. She waited almost a decade to have a child and was told repeatedly to settle for being childless because she didn't have sufficient ovary to produce. But she was also told that she would have children. It was in her blessing and she would not let go of the gift or the promise. She would be a mother!

So she got the gift and maybe she understood somewhere deep inside that there would come an accounting for that gift. It was not that God was a bad or harsh guy or that he desired to see her suffer in later life. It simply means there is an offset for a gift. There is a price placed upon Heaven's greatest gifts as Thomas Paine advised the early Americans.

It cost our Heavenly Father the life of His son to balance the scale for the incalculable gift that was to bring forth His children and let them have agency and live their lives. In giving the gift of life to our mother, God shared in the blessing that these children would be born and experience and live a life in the exact same fashion. That gift would cost a mother being able to see those children grow and see her posterity in this life.

Now I'm sure you ask how this could be possible. It sounds a bit harsh, but God wouldn't inflict his daughter with cancer. That's simply cruel and God is a God of love and allowing His daughter to be a mother was His gift to her because of a promise that had been made, but cancer was not His price for the gift just as crucifixion was not God's choice for His son to die. It simply was.

Science shares a few answers as time goes by. If you know how badly Mom wanted to have children and then having five come in such a short span of years, that is a miracle of huge proportion from a small amount of an ovary. She lived up to the measure of her creation and her desire. The doctors were amazed. Dr. D was amazed and when she announced that she was pregnant, he was determined to do everything he could to grant her this greatest desire.

There was a drug on the market during this time. It was essentially a lab-produced hormone and it was called "Diethylstilbestrol" or DES for short. From 1940 to 1971 DES was given to certain pregnant women in the mistaken belief that it would reduce the risk of pregnancy complication and losses. Mom was at high risk and the doctor wanted her to have every opportunity to carry her children to term since it was a miracle to have gotten pregnant in the first place. If she had a tendency to be a little estrogen-deficient because of the lack of ovary, this DES synthetic hormone would help make up the difference.

Women died from breast and cervical cancer at a high rate in the 1960s. It wasn't as well understood as it would later be and cervical cancer could identify with an HPV virus strain and so forth and could be dealt with. That wasn't the science in 1967 or 1968. It would later be found that

DES was a serious carcinogen. It caused cancer and it caused cervical cancer. Cervical cancer is particularly bad (as is breast cancer) because you can't feel the contagion begin in the cervix where there aren't nerve cells to signal an invasion. There would be later symptoms, but by then the cancer had metastasized to neighboring areas or bone and there is little hope for a remission.

So in reality, the fact that she was granted children and carried them to birth was the very thing that killed her. Do you think she would have wanted it any different? She gave her life that we could live and I often wonder if she knew somewhere in those latter months that the price was going to be called due. It was not because of a harsh God, it was because that was the requirement as surely as a Christ had to elect to give us life by His choosing death.

There was a peace delivered at that Christmas season in 1967. I believe that her angel mother and others were there to bear her up and they were there to welcome her home. Those children who are part of the miracle have no excuse to hang their heads as victims and that they were dealt with in such a manner and without any fault of their own. They were the recipients of an act of love wherein "Greater love hath no (mom) than this, that a (mom) lay down (her) life for (her) (children.)"

Lift up your heads and rally to the legacy. Which one of you wouldn't give your life for your children? I have seen great sacrifices from you on their behalf. At the same time, I have seen that some have made themselves victims of circumstances that they didn't choose. Tough love, folks; she died that you might live. The literal seeds of death were taken into her while we struggled to have life and precisely so that we might have life.

Printed in the USA
CPSIA information can be obtained
at www.ICGtesting.com
JSHW040400210124
55210JS00008B/35